pro vocal

BETTER THAN KARAOKE!

SONGBOOK & SOUND-ALIKE CD
WITH UNIQUE *PITCH-CHANGER*™

VOLUME 62

TOP DOWNLOADS

FOR FEMALE SINGERS

ISBN 978-1-4803-6060-0

HAL•LEONARD® CORPORATION

7777 W. BLUEMOUND RD. P.O. BOX 13819 MILWAUKEE, WI 53213

Visit Hal Leonard Online at
www.halleonard.com

TOP DOWNLOADS
FOR FEMALE SINGERS

Call Me Maybe

Words and Music by Carly Rae Jepsen, Joshua Ramsay and Tavish Crowe

Chorus

so call me may-be. Hey, I just met __ you, and this is cra - zy,

but here's my num-ber, so call me may-be. And all the oth - er boys __

__ try to chase __ me, but here's my num-ber, so call me may-be.

Outro

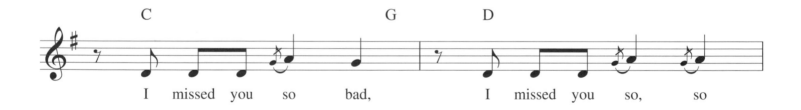

Be - fore you came in - to my life, I missed you so bad,

I missed you so bad, I missed you so, so

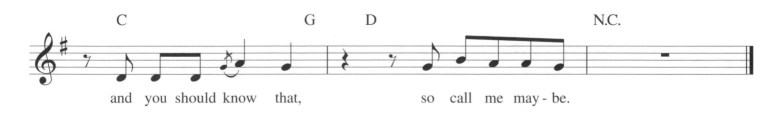

bad. Be - fore you came in - to my life, I missed you so bad,

and you should know that, so call me may - be.

Cups
(When I'm Gone)

from the Motion Picture Soundtrack PITCH PERFECT
Words and Music by A.P. Carter, Luisa Gerstein and Heloise Tunstall-Behrens

Intro
Rhythmically

Verse

I got my tick - et for the long ___ way 'round, ___

two bot - tle o' whis - key for the way. ___ And I

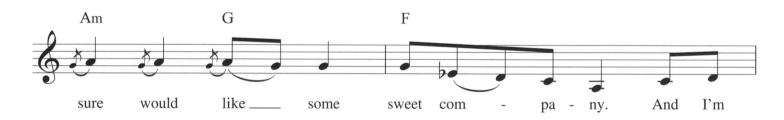

sure would like ___ some sweet com - pa - ny. And I'm

leav - in' to - mor - row, whad - dy - a say? When I'm

Chorus

gone, when I'm go - o - one, you're gon - na miss ___ me when I'm

G   Am   G   F

gone.   You're gon-na miss me by my hair, __ you'll miss me ev-'ry - where, __ oh,

Dm   G   C   Am

you're gon-na miss __ me when I'm gone.   When I'm gone,   when I'm

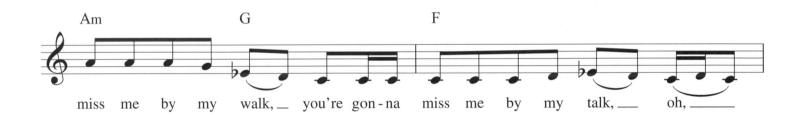

F   Am   G

gone, _____   you're gon-na miss __ me when I'm gone.   You're gon-na

Am   G   F

miss me by my walk, __ you're gon-na miss me by my talk, __ oh, _____

Dm   G   C

you're gon-na miss __ me when I'm gone.

Verse

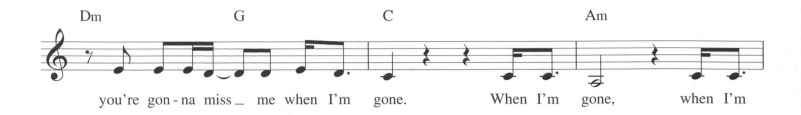

I got my tick - et for the long way 'round, _____

10

F   C

_____ the one with the pret-ti-est of views. It's got

Am   G   F

moun-tains, it's got riv-ers, it's got sights to give you shiv-ers, ____ but it

Am   G   C

sure would __ be pret-ti-er ____ with you. When I'm

Chorus

Am   F   Am

gone, when I'm go - one, __ you're gon-na miss __ me when I'm

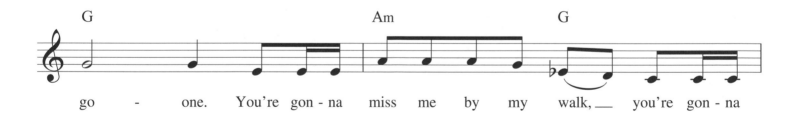

G   Am   G

go - one. You're gon-na miss me by my walk, ___ you're gon-na

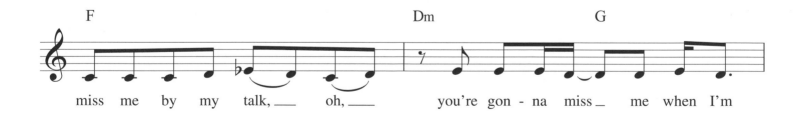

F   Dm   G

miss me by my talk, ___ oh, ___ you're gon-na miss __ me when I'm

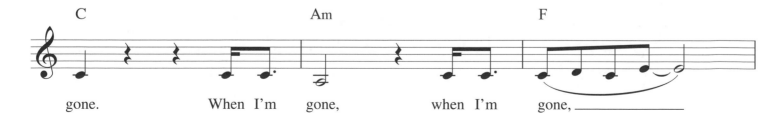

C   Am   F

gone. When I'm gone, when I'm gone, _____

you're gon - na miss _ me when I'm gone.   You're gon - na

miss me by my hair, _ you're gon - na miss me ev - 'ry - where, _ oh yes,

you're gon - na miss _ me when I'm gone.   When I'm

gone,   when I'm gone, _____ you're gon - na miss _ me when I'm

gone.   You're gon - na miss me by my walk, _ you're gon - na

miss me by my talk, _ oh, _ you're gon - na miss _ me when I'm gone.

Heart Attack

**Words and Music by Demi Lovato, Jason Evigan, Mitch Allan,
Aaron Phillips, Sean Douglas and Nikki Williams**

Intro

Moderate Pop

Put-tin' my de-fen-ses up, 'cause I don't wan-na fall in love. If I

ev - er did that, I think I'd have a heart at - tack.

Verse

Nev-er put my love_ out on the line, nev-er said yes to the right guy.

Nev-er had trou-ble get-ting what I want, but when it comes to you, I'm nev-er good e-nough.

When I_____ don't care, _____ I can play 'em like a Ken doll.

Won't wash_ my hair, _____ then make 'em bounce like a bas - ket-ball.

But you make me wan-na act like a girl, _ paint my nails and wear high

heels. __ Yes, you make me so ner-vous, and I just can't hold your hand. __ You make me

Chorus

glow, _____ but I cov-er up. Won't let __ it

show. _____ So I'm

put-tin' my de-fens-es up, 'cause I don't wan-na fall in love. If I

ev-er did that, I think I'd have a heart at - tack. _____

__ I think I'd have a heart at - tack. _____

Verse

__ I think I'd have a heart at - tack. __ Nev-er break a sweat for the oth-er guys.

When you come a - round, I get par-a-lyzed. And ev-'ry time I try to be my-self, __

tack. _____ I think I'd have a heart at -

tack. _____ I think I'd have a heart at -

Bridge

tack. The feel-ings got lost in my lungs. They're burn - ing, I'd

rath - er be numb. And there's no ____ one ____ else to blame. _

____ So scared, I take off in a run. I'm fly - ing too

close to the sun, and I burst in - to flames. _____

Chorus

_____ You make me glow, _____

16

but I cov - er up. Won't let __ it show. _____

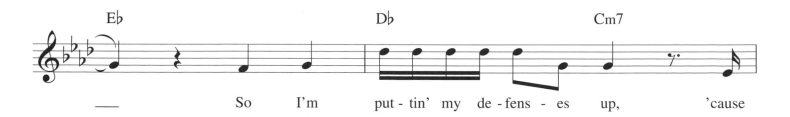

So I'm put - tin' my de - fens - es up, 'cause

I don't wan - na fall in love. If I ev - er did that, I think I'd have a heart at -

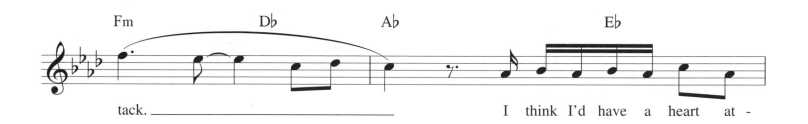

tack. _____ I think I'd have a heart at -

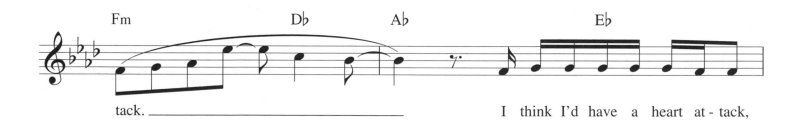

tack. _____ I think I'd have a heart at - tack,

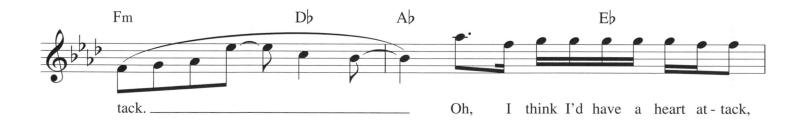

tack. _____ Oh, I think I'd have a heart at - tack,

tack. _____ I think I'd have a heart at - tack. __

Just Give Me a Reason

Words and Music by Alecia Moore, Jeff Bhasker and Nate Ruess

head is run-ning wild a-gain. My dear, we still have ev-'ry-thing, and

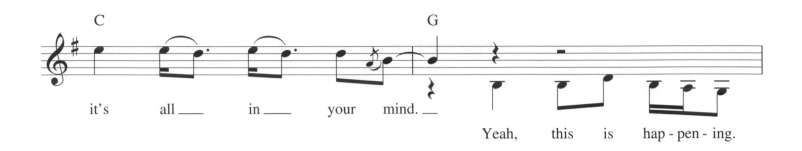

it's all ___ in ___ your mind. ___ Yeah, this is hap-pen-ing.

You've been hav-ing real bad ___ dreams. Oh, oh, you still lie so close to ___

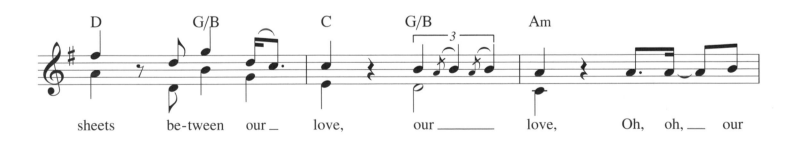

Male: / *Female:*

me. Oh, oh, there's noth-ing more than emp - ty ___

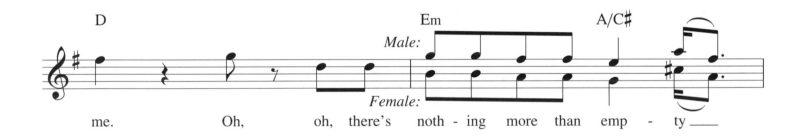

sheets be-tween our ___ love, our ___ love, Oh, oh, ___ our

Chorus

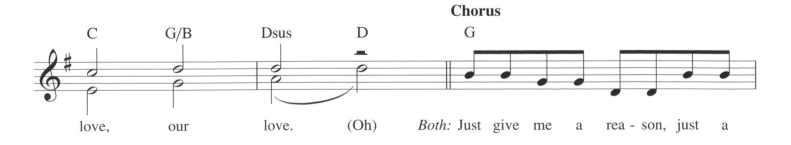

love, our love. (Oh) *Both:* Just give me a rea - son, just a

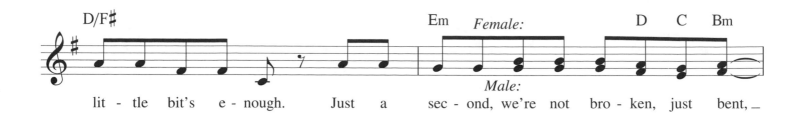

lit - tle bit's e - nough.   Just   a   sec - ond, we're not bro - ken, just bent, __

__   and   we   can   learn   to   love   a - gain. ___   I   nev - er   stopped,   you're   still

writ - ten   in   the   scars   on   my   heart. ___   You're   not   bro - ken, just   bent, __

Bridge

__   and   we   can   learn   to   love   a - gain. ___   *Female:* Oh, ___   tear   ducts   and   rust. __

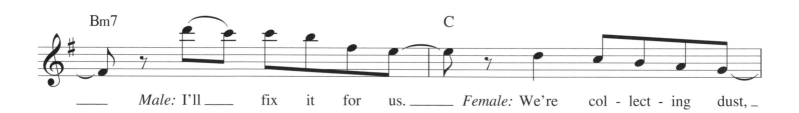

__   *Male:* I'll ___   fix   it   for   us. ___   *Female:* We're   col - lect - ing   dust, _

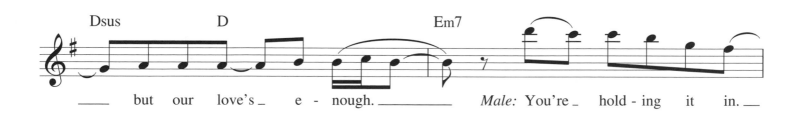

__   but   our   love's _   e - nough. ___   *Male:* You're _   hold - ing   it   in. __

__   *Female:* You're   pour - ing   a   drink. ___   *Male:* No,   noth - ing   is   as

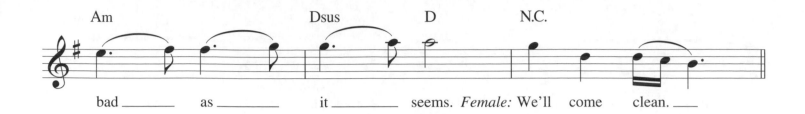

bad _____ as _____ it _____ seems. *Female:* We'll come clean. _____

Chorus

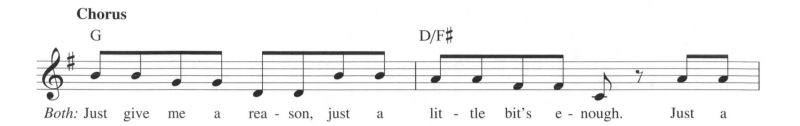

Both: Just give me a rea - son, just a lit - tle bit's e - nough. Just a

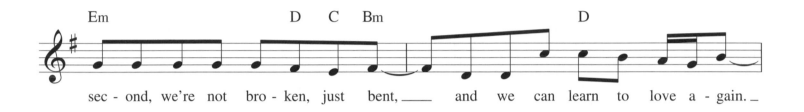

sec - ond, we're not bro - ken, just bent, _____ and we can learn to love a - gain. _

_____ It's in the stars, it's been writ - ten in the scars on our hearts. _

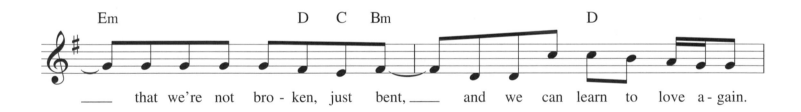

_____ that we're not bro - ken, just bent, _____ and we can learn to love a - gain.

Just give me a rea - son, just a lit - tle bit's e - nough. Just a

sec - ond, we're not bro - ken, just bent, _____ and we can learn to love a - gain. _

It's in the stars, it's been writ-ten in the scars on our hearts. __

that we're not bro-ken, just bent, ____ and we can learn to love a-gain. __

Female: Oh, _____ we can learn to love a-gain. __

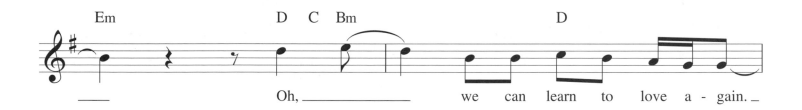

Oh, _____ we can learn to love a-gain. __

Oh, _____ that we're not bro-ken, just bent, __

Outro

__ and we can learn to love a-gain. ____

Skyfall

from the Motion Picture SKYFALL
Words and Music by Adele Adkins and Paul Epworth

Stay

Words and Music by Mikky Ekko and Justin Parker

Intro
With motion

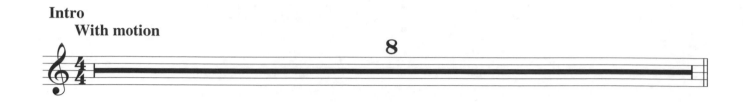

Verse

Female: All a - long, __ it was a fe - ver,

a cold __ sweat, hot - head - ed be - liev - er.

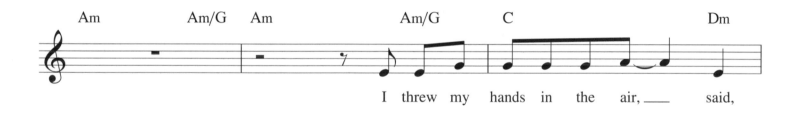

I threw my hands in the air, ___ said,

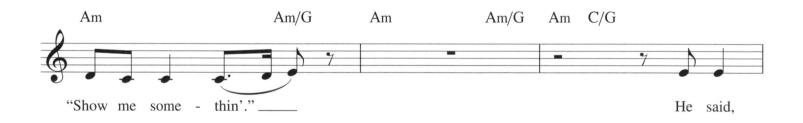

"Show me some - thin'." ____ He said,

"If you dare, __ come a lit - tle clos - er."

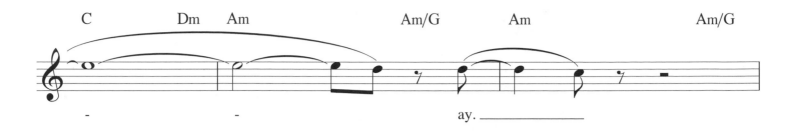

C   Dm   Am   Am/G   Am   Am/G

\-   \-   ay. _____

Bridge

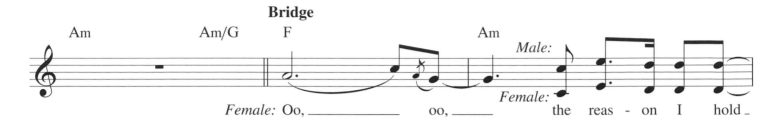

Am   Am/G   F   Am

Male:

Female:

Female: Oo, _____ oo, _____ the reas - on I hold __

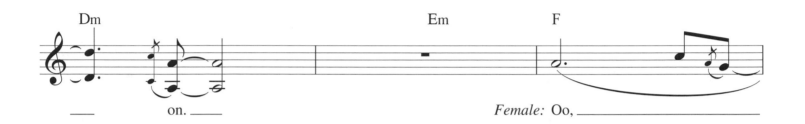

Dm   Em   F

___   on. ___   *Female:* Oo, _____

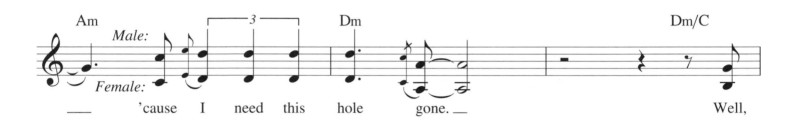

Am   3   Dm   Dm/C

Male:

Female: ___ 'cause I need this hole gone. ___   Well,

Dm   3   F

fun - ny you're the bro - ken one, __ but I'm the on - ly one who need - ed

Am   Dm   3

sav - in'.   'Cause when you nev - er see the light, __ it's

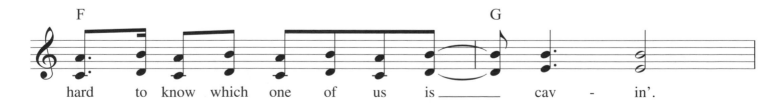

F   G

hard to know which one of us is _____ cav - in'.

Chorus

Female: Not real - ly sure how to feel a - bout _ it. Some-

- thin' in the way you _ move _ makes _ me feel like I can't

Male:

Female:

live with - out you. It _____ takes me all the way. _

Female: I want you to stay. _____

Stay. _____

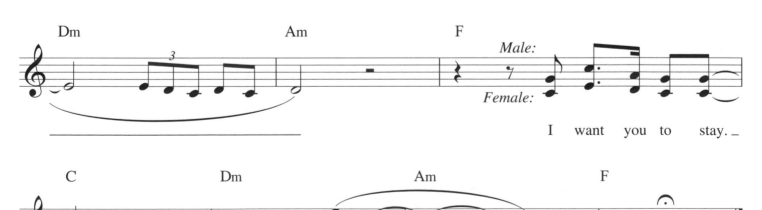

I want you to stay. _

Male:

Female:

Female: Oo. _____

32

A Thousand Years

from the Summit Entertainment film THE TWILIGHT SAGA: BREAKING DAWN – PART 1
Words and Music by David Hodges and Christina Perri

Verse

Time stands still, beau-ty in all she is. I will be brave, I will not let an-y-thing take a-way what's stand-ing in front of me. Ev-e-ry breath, ev-e-ry hour has come to this. One step clos - er.

Chorus

I have died ev-'ry day, wait-ing for you.

Dar-lin', don't be a-fraid, I have loved you for a

thou - sand years. I'll love you for a

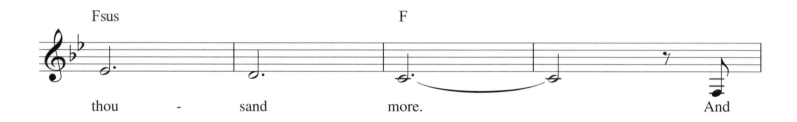

thou - sand more. And

all a-long I be-lieved I would find you.

Time has brought your heart to me. I have loved you for a

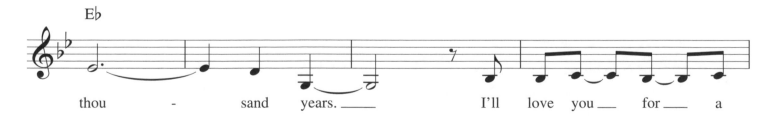

thou - sand years. I'll love you for a

Fsus   F

thou - sand   more. _____

Interlude

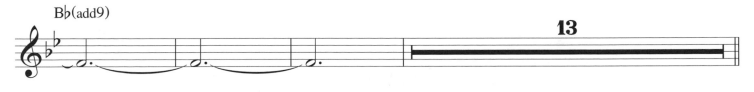

B♭(add9)

13

Bridge

Cm7

One   step

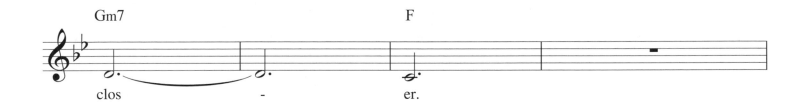

Gm7   F

clos - er.

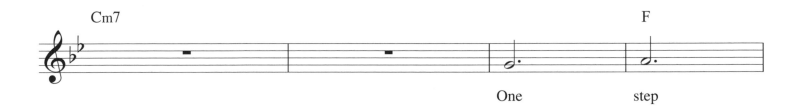

Cm7   F

One   step

Gm7   F/A

clos - er.

Chorus

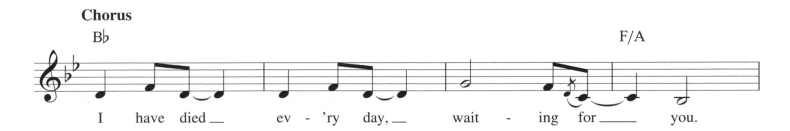

B♭   F/A

I   have   died __ ev - 'ry   day, __ wait - ing   for _____ you.

22

Words and Music by Taylor Swift, Shellback and Max Martin

night's the night __ when we for-get a-bout the dead - lines, it's time. __

Chorus

__ Uh-oh. I don't know a-bout you, but I'm feel-in' twen-ty two. __

Ev-'ry-thing will be al - right if you keep me next to you. _____

_____ You don't know a-bout me, but I'll bet you want __ to. ____

Ev-'ry-thing will be al - right if we just keep danc - in' like we're __

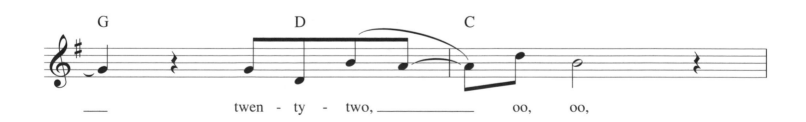

__ twen - ty - two, _____ oo, oo,

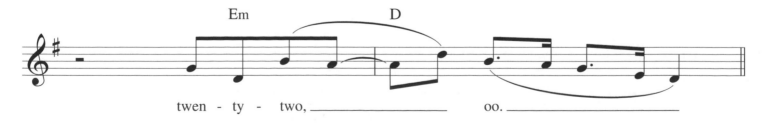

twen - ty - two, _____ oo. _____

Verse

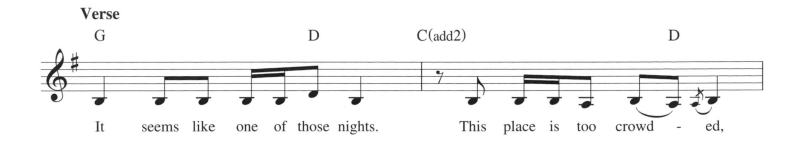

It seems like one of those nights. This place is too crowd - ed,

too man - y cool ___ kids, uh - uh. uh - uh.

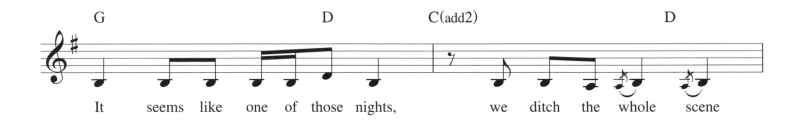

It seems like one of those nights, we ditch the whole scene

and end up dream - in' in - stead of sleep - in'. Yeah, _____ we're

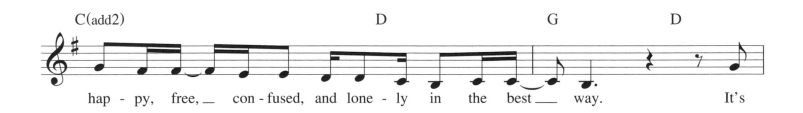

hap - py, free, __ con - fused, and lone - ly in the best __ way. It's

mis - 'ra - ble ___ and mag - i - cal. Oh, ___ yeah, _____ to -

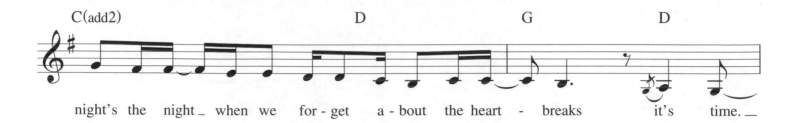

night's the night _ when we for-get a-bout the heart - breaks it's time. _

Chorus

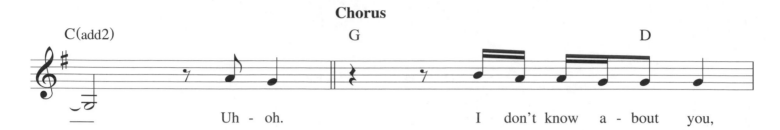

_ Uh - oh. I don't know a-bout you,

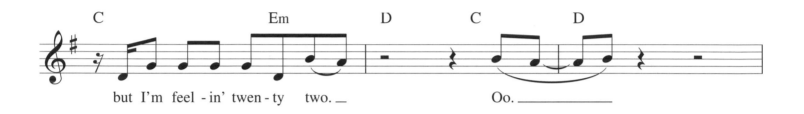

but I'm feel-in' twen-ty two. _ Oo. _____

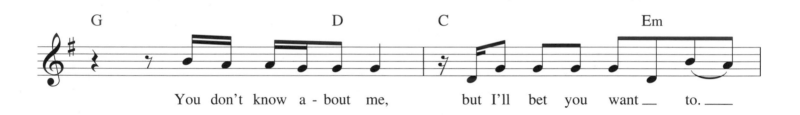

You don't know a-bout me, but I'll bet you want _ to. _____

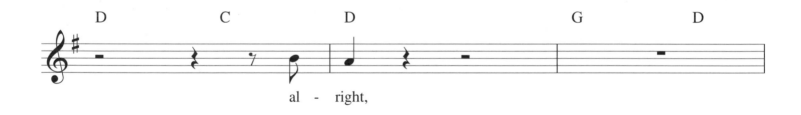

al - right,

Oh, oh, oh, oh, oh. I don't know a-bout

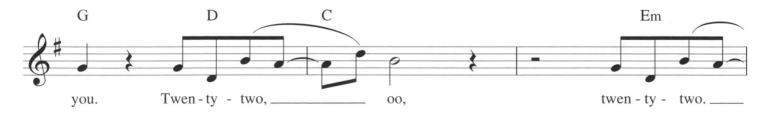

you. Twen-ty - two, _____ oo, twen-ty - two. _____

Bridge

we ditch the whole scene.

we won't be sleep - in' ____

you look like bad news, I got - ta have you, I got - ta have you. ____

Oh, _____ oo,

Chorus

yeah, _____ I don't

know a - bout you. ____ Oo. _____

You don't know a - bout me. ____

Just like we're twen-ty-two, ___ oo. ___

___ To - night.

Oh, yeah, yeah, ___ oh, yeah, yeah, ___ yeah.

We ditch the whole scene.

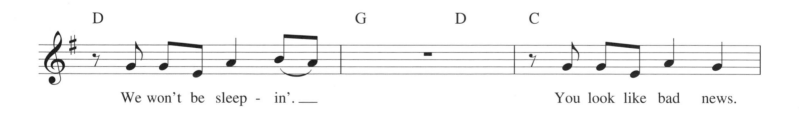

We won't be sleep - in'. ___ You look like bad news.

I got - ta have you, I got - ta have you. ___

ORIGINAL KEYS FOR SINGERS

ACROSS THE UNIVERSE
Because • Blackbird • Hey Jude • Let It Be • Revolution • Something • and more.
00307010 Vocal Transcriptions with Piano $19.95

LOUIS ARMSTRONG
Dream a Little Dream of Me • Hello, Dolly! • Mack the Knife • Makin' Whoopee! • Mame • St. Louis Blues • What a Wonderful World • Zip-A-Dee-Doo-Dah • and more.
00307029 Vocal Transcriptions with Piano $19.99

THE BEATLES
And I Love Her • Blackbird • The Fool on the Hill • Here, There and Everywhere • I Will • Let It Be • Michelle • Something • With a Little Help from My Friends • and more.
00307400 Vocal Transcriptions with Piano $19.99

BROADWAY HITS (FEMALE SINGERS)
23 Broadway favorites from their most memorable renditions, including: And I Am Telling You I'm Not Going (Jennifer Hudson) • Cabaret (Liza Minelli) • Defying Gravity (Idina Menzel) • Edelweiss (Julie Andrews) • and more.
00119085 Vocal Transcriptions with Piano $19.99

BROADWAY HITS (MALE SINGERS)
23 timeless Broadway hits true to the men who made them famous: Bring Him Home (David Campbell) • If Ever I Would Leave You (Robert Goulet) • Oh, What a Beautiful Mornin' (Gordon MacRae) • and more.
00119084 Vocal Transcriptions with Piano $19.99

MARIAH CAREY
Always Be My Baby • Dreamlover • Emotions • Heartbreaker • Hero • I Don't Wanna Cry • Love Takes Time • Loverboy • One Sweet Day • Vision of Love • We Belong Together • and more.
00306835 Vocal Transcriptions with Piano $19.95

PATSY CLINE
Always • Blue Moon of Kentucky • Crazy • Faded Love • I Fall to Pieces • Just a Closer Walk with Thee • Sweet Dreams • more. Also includes a biography.
00740072 Vocal Transcriptions with Piano $16.99

ELLA FITZGERALD
A-tisket, A-tasket • But Not for Me • Easy to Love • Embraceable You • The Lady Is a Tramp • Misty • Oh, Lady Be Good! • Satin Doll • Stompin' at the Savoy • Take the "A" Train • and more. Includes a biography and discography.
00740252 Vocal Transcriptions with Piano $16.95

JOSH GROBAN
Alejate • Awake • Believe • February Song • In Her Eyes • Now or Never • O Holy Night • Per Te • The Prayer • To Where You Are • Un Amore Per Sempre • Un Dia Llegara • You Are Loved (Don't Give Up) • You Raise Me Up • You're Still You • and more.
00306969 Vocal Transcriptions with Piano $19.99

GREAT FEMALE SINGERS
Cry Me a River (Ella Fitzgerald) • Crazy (Patsy Cline) • Fever (Peggy Lee) • How Deep Is the Ocean (How High Is the Sky) (Billie Holiday) • Little Girl Blue (Nina Simone) • Tenderly (Rosemary Clooney) • and more.
00307132 Vocal Transcriptions with Piano $19.99

GREAT MALE SINGERS
Can't Help Falling in Love (Elvis Presley) • Georgia on My Mind (Ray Charles) • I've Got the World on a String (Frank Sinatra) • Mona Lisa (Nat King Cole) • Ol' Man River (Paul Robeson) • What a Wonderful World (Louis Armstrong) • and more.
00307133 Vocal Transcriptions with Piano $19.99

BILLIE HOLIDAY
TRANSCRIBED FROM HISTORIC RECORDINGS
Billie's Blues (I Love My Man) • Body and Soul • Crazy He Calls Me • Easy Living • A Fine Romance • God Bless' the Child • Lover, Come Back to Me • Miss Brown to You • Strange Fruit • The Very Thought of You • and more.
00740140 Vocal Transcriptions with Piano $17.99

JAZZ DIVAS
A collection of 30 ballads recorded by Ella Fitzgerald, Billie Holiday, Diana Krall, Nina Simone, Sarah Vaughan, and more! Includes: Black Coffee • It Might as Well Be Spring • The Man I Love • My Funny Valentine • and more.
00114959 Vocal Transcriptions with Piano $19.99

LADIES OF CHRISTMAS
Grown-Up Christmas List (Amy Grant) • Hard Candy Christmas (Dolly Parton) • Merry Christmas, Darling (Karen Carpenter) • Rockin' Around the Christmas Tree (Brenda Lee) • Santa Baby (Eartha Kitt) • and more.
00312192 Vocal Transcriptions with Piano $19.99

NANCY LAMOTT
Autumn Leaves • Downtown • I Have Dreamed • It Might as Well Be Spring • Moon River • Skylark • That Old Black Magic • and more.
00306995 Vocal Transcriptions with Piano $19.99

LEONA LEWIS – SPIRIT
Better in Time • Bleeding Love • The First Time Ever I Saw Your Face • Here I Am • Homeless • I Will Be • I'm You • Whatever It Takes • Yesterday • and more.
00307007 Vocal Transcriptions with Piano $17.95

CHRIS MANN
Always on My Mind • Ave Maria • Cuore • Falling • Longer • My Way • Need You Now • On a Night like This • Roads • Unless You Mean It • Viva La Vida.
00118921 Vocal Transcriptions with Piano $16.99

MEN OF CHRISTMAS
The Christmas Song (Chestnuts Roasting on an Open Fire) (Nat King Cole) • A Holly Jolly Christmas (Burl Ives) • It's Beginning to Look like Christmas (Perry Como) • White Christmas (Bing Crosby) • and more.
00312241 Vocal Transcriptions with Piano $19.99

THE BETTE MIDLER SONGBOOK
Boogie Woogie Bugle Boy • Friends • From a Distance • The Glory of Love • The Rose • Some People's Lives • Stay with Me • Stuff like That There • Ukulele Lady • The Wind Beneath My Wings • and more, plus a fantastic bio and photos.
00307067 Vocal Transcriptions with Piano $19.99

THE BEST OF LIZA MINNELLI
And All That Jazz • Cabaret • Losing My Mind • Maybe This Time • Me and My Baby • Theme from "New York, New York" • Ring Them Bells • Sara Lee • Say Liza (Liza with a Z) • Shine It On • Sing Happy • The Singer • Taking a Chance on Love.
00306928 Vocal Transcriptions with Piano $19.99

ONCE
All the Way Down • Broken Hearted Hoover Fixer Sucker Guy • Fallen from the Sky • Falling Slowly • Gold • The Hill • If You Want Me • Leave • Lies • Once • Say It to Me Now • Trying to Pull Myself Away • When Your Mind's Made Up.
00102569 Vocal Transcriptions with Piano $16.99

FRANK SINATRA – MORE OF HIS BEST
Almost like Being in Love • Cheek to Cheek • Fly Me to the Moon • I Could Write a Book • It Might as Well Be Spring • Luck Be a Lady • Old Devil Moon • Somebody Loves Me • When the World Was Young • and more.
00307081 Vocal Transcriptions with Piano $19.99

THE VERY BEST OF FRANK SINATRA
Come Fly with Me • I've Got You Under My Skin • It Was a Very Good Year • My Way • Night and Day • Summer Wind • The Way You Look Tonight • You Make Me Feel So Young • and more. Includes biography.
00306753 Vocal Transcriptions with Piano $19.95

STEVE TYRELL – BACK TO BACHARACH
Alfie • Always Something There to Remind Me • Close to You • I Say a Little Prayer • The Look of Love • Raindrops Keep Fallin' on My Head • This Guy's in Love with You • Walk on By • and more.
00307024 Vocal Transcriptions with Piano $16.99

THE BEST OF STEVE TYRELL
Ain't Misbehavin' • I Concentrate on You • I've Got a Crush on You • Isn't It Romantic? • A Kiss to Build a Dream On • Stardust • You'd Be So Nice to Come Home To • and more.
00307027 Vocal Transcriptions with Piano $16.99

SARAH VAUGHAN
Black Coffee • If You Could See Me Now • It Might as Well Be Spring • My Funny Valentine • The Nearness of You • A Night in Tunisia • Perdido • September Song • Tenderly • and more.
00306558 Vocal Transcriptions with Piano $17.95

VOCAL POP
Bad Romance • Bleeding Love • Breathe • Don't Know Why • Halo • I Will Always Love You • If I Ain't Got You • Rehab • Rolling in the Deep • Teenage Dream • You Belong with Me • and more!
00312656 Vocal Transcriptions with Piano $19.99

ANDY WILLIAMS – CHRISTMAS COLLECTION
Blue Christmas • Do You Hear What I Hear • Happy Holiday • The Little Drummer Boy • O Holy Night • Sleigh Ride • What Are You Doing New Year's Eve? • and more. Includes a great bio!
00307158 Vocal Transcriptions with Piano $17.99

ANDY WILLIAMS
Can't Get Used to Losing You • The Days of Wine and Roses • The Hawaiian Wedding Song (Ke Kali Nei Au) • The Impossible Dream • Moon River • More • The Most Wonderful Time of the Year • Red Roses for a Blue Lady • Speak Softly, Love • A Time for Us • Where Do I Begin • and more.
00307160 Vocal Transcriptions with Piano $17.99

HAL•LEONARD® CORPORATION
7777 W. BLUEMOUND RD. P.O. BOX 13819 MILWAUKEE, WI 53213

pro Vocal®
BETTER THAN KARAOKE!

Pro Vocal® Series
SONGBOOK & SOUND-ALIKE CD
SING GREAT SONGS WITH A PROFESSIONAL BAND

Whether you're a karaoke singer or an auditioning professional, the Pro Vocal® series is for you! Unlike most karaoke packs, each book in the Pro Vocal Series contains the lyrics, melody, and chord symbols for at least eight hit songs. The CD contains demos for listening, and separate backing tracks so you can sing along. The CD is playable on any CD player, but it is also enhanced so PC and Mac computer users can adjust the recording to any pitch without changing the tempo! Perfect for home rehearsal, parties, auditions, corporate events, and gigs without a backup band.

WOMEN'S EDITIONS
00740247	1. Broadway Songs	$14.95
00740249	2. Jazz Standards	$15.99
00740246	3. Contemporary Hits	$14.95
00740277	4. '80s Gold	$12.95
00740299	5. Christmas Standards	$15.95
00740281	6. Disco Fever	$12.95
00740279	7. R&B Super Hits	$12.95
00740309	8. Wedding Gems	$12.95
00740409	9. Broadway Standards	$14.95
00740348	10. Andrew Lloyd Webber	$14.95
00740344	11. Disney's Best	$15.99
00740378	12. Ella Fitzgerald	$14.95
00740350	14. Musicals of Boublil & Schönberg	$14.95
00740377	15. Kelly Clarkson	$14.95
00740342	16. Disney Favorites	$15.99
00740353	17. Jazz Ballads	$14.95
00740376	18. Jazz Vocal Standards	$17.99
00740375	20. Hannah Montana	$16.95
00740354	21. Jazz Favorites	$14.99
00740374	22. Patsy Cline	$14.95
00740369	23. Grease	$14.95
00740367	25. Mamma Mia	$15.99
00740365	26. Movie Songs	$14.95
00740360	28. High School Musical 1 & 2	$14.95
00740363	29. Torch Songs	$14.95
00740379	30. Hairspray	$15.99
00740380	31. Top Hits	$14.95
00740384	32. Hits of the '70s	$14.95
00740388	33. Billie Holiday	$14.95
00740389	34. The Sound of Music	$16.99
00740390	35. Contemporary Christian	$14.95
00740392	36. Wicked	$17.99
00740393	37. More Hannah Montana	$14.95
00740396	39. Christmas Hits	$15.95
00740410	40. Broadway Classics	$14.95
00740415	41. Broadway Favorites	$14.99
00740416	42. Great Standards You Can Sing	$14.99
00740417	43. Singable Standards	$14.99
00740418	44. Favorite Standards	$14.99
00740419	45. Sing Broadway	$14.99
00740420	46. More Standards	$14.99
00740421	47. Timeless Hits	$14.99
00740422	48. Easygoing R&B	$14.99
00740424	49. Taylor Swift	$16.99
00740425	50. From This Moment On	$14.99
00740426	51. Great Standards Collection	$19.99
00740430	52. Worship Favorites	$14.99
00740434	53. Lullabyes	$14.99
00740438	54. Lady Gaga	$14.99
00740444	55. Amy Winehouse	$15.99
00740445	56. Adele	$16.99
00740446	57. The Grammy Awards Best Female Pop Vocal Performance 1990-1999	$14.99
00740447	58. The Grammy Awards Best Female Pop Vocal Performance 2000-2009	$14.99
00109374	60. Katy Perry	$14.99
00116334	61. Taylor Swift Hits	$14.99
00123120	62. Top Downloads	$14.99

MEN'S EDITIONS
00740250	2. Jazz Standards	$14.95
00740278	4. '80s Gold	$12.95
00740298	5. Christmas Standards	$15.95
00740280	6. R&B Super Hits	$12.95
00740282	7. Disco Fever	$12.95
00740310	8. Wedding Gems	$12.95
00740411	9. Broadway Greats	$14.99
00740333	10. Elvis Presley – Volume 1	$14.95
00740349	11. Andrew Lloyd Webber	$14.99
00740345	12. Disney's Best	$14.95
00740347	13. Frank Sinatra Classics	$14.95
00740334	14. Lennon & McCartney	$14.99
00740453	15. Queen	$14.99
00740335	16. Elvis Presley – Volume 2	$14.99
00740343	17. Disney Favorites	$14.99
00740351	18. Musicals of Boublil & Schönberg	$14.95
00740337	19. Lennon & McCartney – Volume 2	$14.99
00740346	20. Frank Sinatra Standards	$14.95
00740338	21. Lennon & McCartney – Volume 3	$14.99
00740358	22. Great Standards	$14.99
00740336	23. Elvis Presley	$14.99
00740341	24. Duke Ellington	$14.99
00740339	25. Lennon & McCartney – Volume 4	$14.99
00740359	26. Pop Standards	$14.99
00740362	27. Michael Bublé	$15.99
00740454	28. Maroon 5	$14.99
00740364	29. Torch Songs	$14.95
00740366	30. Movie Songs	$14.95
00740368	31. Hip Hop Hits	$14.95
00740370	32. Grease	$14.95
00740371	33. Josh Groban	$14.95
00740373	34. Billy Joel	$14.99
00740381	35. Hits of the '50s	$14.95
00740382	36. Hits of the '60s	$14.95
00740383	37. Hits of the '70s	$14.95
00740385	38. Motown	$14.95
00740386	39. Hank Williams	$14.95
00740387	40. Neil Diamond	$14.95
00740391	41. Contemporary Christian	$14.95
00740397	42. Christmas Hits	$15.95
00740399	43. Ray	$14.95
00740400	44. The Rat Pack Hits	$14.99
00740401	45. Songs in the Style of Nat "King" Cole	$14.99
00740402	46. At the Lounge	$14.95
00740403	47. The Big Band Singer	$14.95
00740404	48. Jazz Cabaret Songs	$14.99
00740405	49. Cabaret Songs	$14.99
00740406	50. Big Band Standards	$14.99
00740412	51. Broadway's Best	$14.99
00740427	52. Great Standards Collection	$19.99
00740431	53. Worship Favorites	$14.99
00740435	54. Barry Manilow	$14.99
00740436	55. Lionel Richie	$14.99
00740439	56. Michael Bublé – Crazy Love	$15.99
00740441	57. Johnny Cash	$14.99
00740442	58. Bruno Mars	$14.99
00740448	59. The Grammy Awards Best Male Pop Vocal Performance 1990-1999	$14.99
00740449	60. The Grammy Awards Best Male Pop Vocal Performance 2000-2009	$14.99
00740452	61. Michael Bublé – Call Me Irresponsible	$14.99

00101777	62. Michael Bublé – Christmas	$19.99
00102658	63. Michael Jackson	$14.99
00109288	64. Justin Bieber	$14.99

WARM-UPS
00740395	Vocal Warm-Ups	$14.99

MIXED EDITIONS
These editions feature songs for both male and female voices.
00740311	1. Wedding Duets	$12.95
00740398	2. Enchanted	$14.95
00740407	3. Rent	$14.95
00740408	4. Broadway Favorites	$14.99
00740413	5. South Pacific	$15.99
00740414	6. High School Musical 3	$14.99
00740429	7. Christmas Carols	$14.99
00740437	8. Glee	$16.99
00740440	9. More Songs from Glee	$21.99
00740443	10. Even More Songs from Glee	$15.99
00116960	11. Les Misérables	$19.99

KIDS EDITIONS
00740451	1. Songs Children Can Sing!	$14.99

Visit Hal Leonard online at
www.halleonard.com

HAL•LEONARD®

7777 W. BLUEMOUND RD. P.O. BOX 13819 MILWAUKEE, WI 53213

Prices, contents, & availability subject to change without notice.

1113